Religious Topics

RELIGIOUS BUILDINGS

Jon Mayled

Religious Topics

Birth Customs
Death Customs
Family Life
Feasting and Fasting
Holy Books
Initiation Rites
Marriage Customs

Pilgrimage
Religious Art
Religious Buildings
Religious Dress
Religious Services
Teachers and Prophets

Cover A Buddhist temple in Rangoon, Burma

First published in 1986 by Wayland (Publishers) Limited
61 Western Road, Hove, East Sussex BN3 1JD, England

© Copyright 1986 Wayland (Publishers) Limited

British Library Cataloguing in Publication Data
Mayled, Jon
  Religious buildings. – (Religious topics)
  1. Temples – Juvenile literature   2. Churches
  – Juvenile literature
  I. Title   II. Series
  291.3′   BL586

ISBN 0–85078–952–4

Phototypeset by Kalligraphics Ltd., Redhill, Surrey
Printed in Italy by G. Canale & C.S.p.A., Turin
Bound in Belgium by Casterman S.A.

Contents

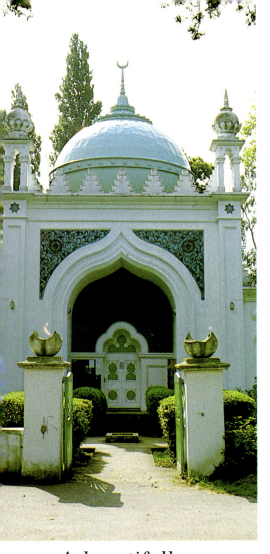

A beautifully decorated mosque in the south of England.

Introduction

If we stand in any town or city and look around us we will see all sorts and types of buildings. There will be old ones and new ones, some ugly and some beautiful. In any street we may see shops, offices, houses and the places of worship of various religious groups. It is sometimes possible to tell which type of religious worship a building is used for simply by looking at its architecture.

The outside of these religious buildings may be very plain or very ornate, depending upon the particular religion. If we enter one of these buildings we may find many different types of art – pictures, statues or stained-glass windows perhaps. These can reflect the beliefs of the religion and can tell us something about the way it has developed over hundreds or thousands of years.

A Buddhist temple in Penang, Malaysia. On the left is the shrine room.

5

Buddhism

Religious buildings, many of them very splendid, can be found in all Buddhist countries. They are often very grandly decorated and filled with works of art. The main place of

The temple of the Emerald Buddha in Bangkok. Buddhist temples are often very grandly decorated.

Buddhist worship is the temple, though most Buddhists will make a shrine somewhere in their homes, with a *buddharupa*, a statue of the Buddha, in pride of place. Most Buddhist temples are built within a monastery or at a particular place associated with the Buddha or his followers. There are two schools of Buddhism: the *Theravada* school and the *Mahayana* school. An important building for *Theravada* Buddhists is a *stupa*. *Stupas* are 'relic chambers' – they contain relics either of the Buddha himself or one of his followers. No one can enter a *stupa*; it is just a monument to commemorate the Buddha and his teachings.

Outside Buddhist temples there is usually a *bo* or fig tree. The Buddha reached a state of enlightenment and understood the way to live life while sitting under a *bo* tree. Wherever possible the trees at Buddhist temples will be grown from cuttings of the original tree.

A Buddhist shrine in a temple in Taiwan. Visitors leave flowers and other gifts in front of the Buddha images in the shrine room.

Buddhist temples are built in five layers to symbolize the five elements of the Buddhist faith: earth, air, fire, water and wisdom.

The most important part of a Buddhist temple, the shrine room, is built to face east. Inside is a statue of the Buddha surrounded by flowers, candles and incense sticks. In front of this statue is a large open area for the worshippers, places for people to make their offerings and a stand for the teacher. In the temple there are often huge prayer wheels with prayers inscribed on them. Worshippers turn these whilst chanting a prayer.

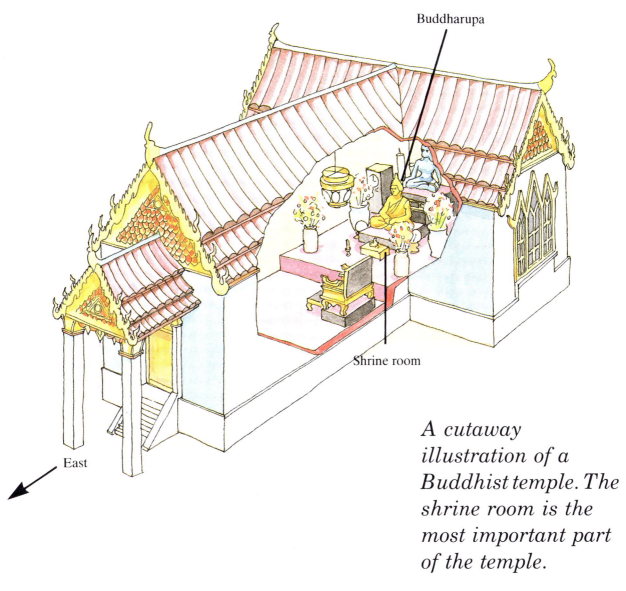

Buddharupa

Shrine room

East

A cutaway illustration of a Buddhist temple. The shrine room is the most important part of the temple.

9

Christianity

Christians of different denominations or groups worship in buildings of varying ages, styles and designs. These may be called churches, chapels, cathedrals, meeting halls or by many other names.

Anglican and Roman Catholic churches are often very impressive buildings. Some are very old whilst others are very modern. The many different styles of building reflect the changes in architectural design which have taken place over centuries. On the outside there is often a tower or spire, which may contain bells used to tell the worshippers that a service, such as a wedding or funeral, is soon to take place. There is usually a cross, the symbol of Christianity, outside too.

Often the building itself is cross-shaped and inside at the head of the cross is the altar. It is here the priest celebrates the Eucharist

The Roman Catholic basilica of Sacré Coeur *in Paris, built in 1876.*

(Holy Communion) in memory of the Last Supper which Jesus ate with his twelve disciples before His death on the cross. The area around the altar is enclosed by the communion rails and is called the sanctuary. Recently, many churches have also built altars in the centre so that the priest can stand in the middle of the congregation.

In front of the sanctuary is the chancel where the choir sits and which also often contains the organ, used to provide music for the service. Sometimes the chancel is separated

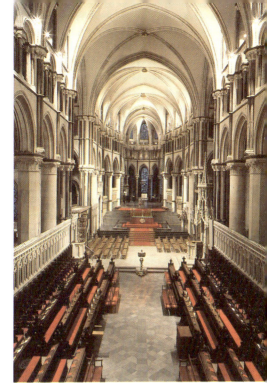

Above *A view of the high altar and choir stalls in Canterbury Cathedral.*

Left *A Methodist church in Hamilton, New Zealand.*

11

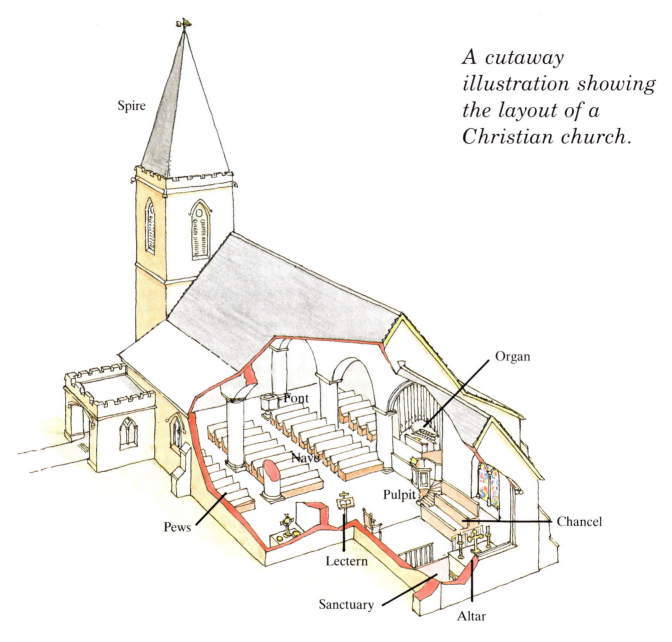

Spire

A cutaway illustration showing the layout of a Christian church.

Organ

Font

Nave

Pulpit

Pews

Chancel

Lectern

Sanctuary

Altar

from the rest of the church by a thin wooden screen called the rood screen through which the worshippers can see the altar. In front of this screen is the pulpit where the priest stands to give his sermon and the lectern, a stand from where the Bible is read during services. The nave, where people sit, is usually full of seats called pews. Somewhere near the west end is the baptistery. This contains the font, a stone or wooden stand holding a bowl of water which is used for baptizing children.

In some churches there are many religious pictures and statues with stands in front on which people can place lighted candles. Some older churches have wall paintings of scenes from the Bible. Stained-glass windows also often tell Bible stories.

In Roman Catholic churches there may be confessional boxes. It is here that people kneel when they tell the priest their sins and ask him for forgiveness through God.

A statue of the Virgin Mary with the baby Jesus in her arms.

Hinduism

A Hindu temple is called a *mandir* – a place of worship. Hindu temples are dedicated to a particular god or gods. They are built so that their entrance faces the rising sun. In the courtyard of the temple there is a statue of the god's vehicle – the animal on which the god is said to ride. So if the temple is dedicated to *Shiva* you would see a statue of *Nandin* the bull.

In India the Hindu temples are usually

A statue of Nandin *the bull, in a* Shiva *temple in India.*

surrounded by a walled enclosure with high porches at the entrances called *gopurams*. These are covered with scenes from Hindu religious stories. There are steps which lead up to the main building. You pass through the entrance gateway *(torana)* into the porch *(ardhamandapa)* and so in to the main room *(mahamandapa)*. Here worshippers remove their shoes as they are considered unclean through having made contact with the earth. At the end of this room is the *garbhagriha*, the shrine of the god or gods. Only the priests can go into this shrine and during the afternoon, when the gods go to sleep, a door or screen is drawn across.

As well as statues the shrine room may also have pictures of other gods. These brightly coloured pictures are also found in many Hindu homes. There may also be a copy of the *Bhagavad Gita*, one of the Hindu Holy Books, and a bottle of Ganges water. There are bells which are rung to attract the gods

A gopuram *at the entrance to a Hindu temple in Sri Lanka.*

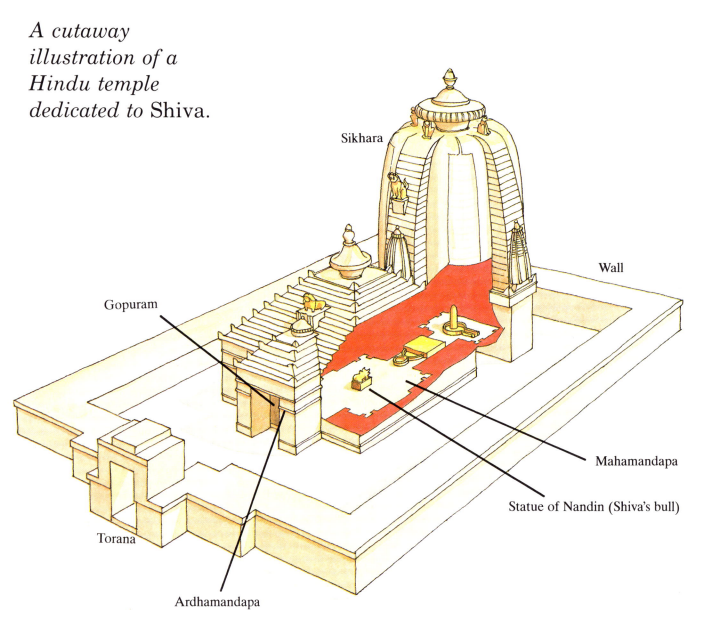

A cutaway illustration of a Hindu temple dedicated to Shiva.

Sikhara

Wall

Gopuram

Mahamandapa

Statue of Nandin (Shiva's bull)

Torana

Ardhamandapa

The Hindu symbol 'OM' on a decorated float during a festival.

attention and slots in which people place money as gifts. On the walls there may be the Sanskrit symbol for 'OM' and the *swastika*, a Hindu symbol of good luck.

Above the shrine is a tower or canopy *(sikhara)* which represents a mountain as these are always holy places to Hindus. It is possible to walk around the shrine in a passageway *(pradakshina)* and often there are processions here on feast days. In a *mandir* in India you would also find a tank or large pool in which the worshippers could wash themselves before entering the temple.

Below Hindu temples are often decorated with statues of their gods.

Islam

Muslims worship together in a mosque which means 'place of prayer or prostration'. Some mosques are very fine examples of Muslim architecture and are beautiful buildings. They usually have two very obvious features: a dome above the main prayer hall which represents the universe, and at least one tall

Muslim mosques usually have a dome and a tall, thin tower called a minaret.

Muslims must face the mihrab *(recess in the wall) when praying as it faces the direction of the* Ka'ba *in the holy city of Mecca.*

thin tower called a *minaret*. It is from the *minaret* that a man known as the *muezzin* calls Muslims to prayer five times a day. In many mosques clock faces are fastened to one of the walls to tell the times of prayer.

Outside the mosque, or near the entrance hall, will be a place with running water where the worshippers can perform the ritual of washing, *wudu*, which is necessary before praying. There are no seats in the main prayer hall, instead there are rugs or carpets on the floor. One wall is called the *qibla* which means 'direction', as it faces in the direction of the *Ka'ba* in the holy city of Mecca in Saudi Arabia. In the middle of the *qibla* is a recess called the *mihrab* and Muslims must face this direction when praying. To the right of the *mihrab* is a small pulpit called the *minbar* where the *Imam* stands when giving the Friday sermon, *khutba*.

No religious statues or pictures are allowed in mosques and instead the walls are often very richly decorated with patterns of flowers and geometric designs. Amongst these will be inscriptions from the *Qur'an*, the Muslim Holy Book, written in Arabic together with the names of *Allah* and Muhammad. There will also be part of the mosque which is screened off for use by the women. They can hear what is happening but cannot be seen.

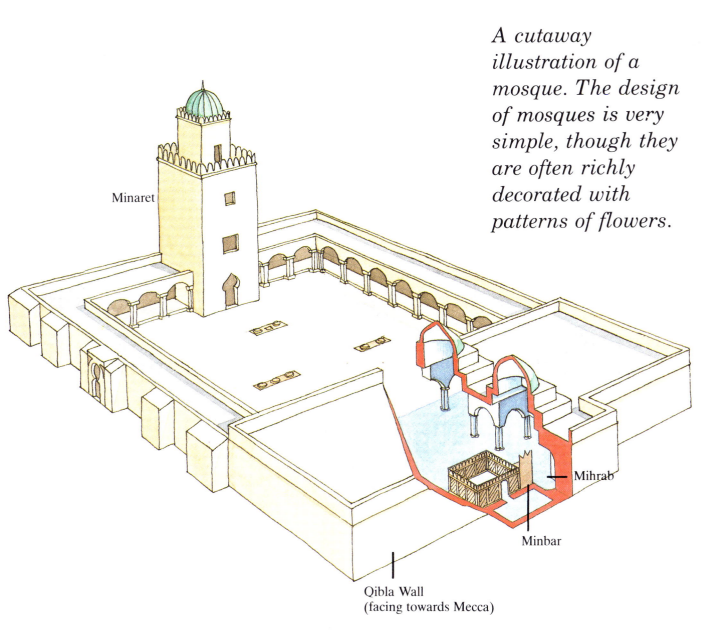

Minaret

A cutaway illustration of a mosque. The design of mosques is very simple, though they are often richly decorated with patterns of flowers.

Mihrab

Minbar

Qibla Wall
(facing towards Mecca)

21

Judaism

The Jewish place of worship is the synagogue. From the outside these are often very plain buildings and may be noticeable only by the Star of David, the six-pointed star, and an inscription in Hebrew.

Inside, the centre of the main wall, facing east towards Jerusalem, contains a decorated cupboard – the Ark. This holds the scrolls on which are hand-written in Hebrew the *Torah*, the first five books of the *Tenakh*, the Jewish Holy Scriptures. These scrolls often have very elaborate cases of velvet or silk, richly

The Torah *scrolls are kept in the Ark, which is a curtained alcove.*

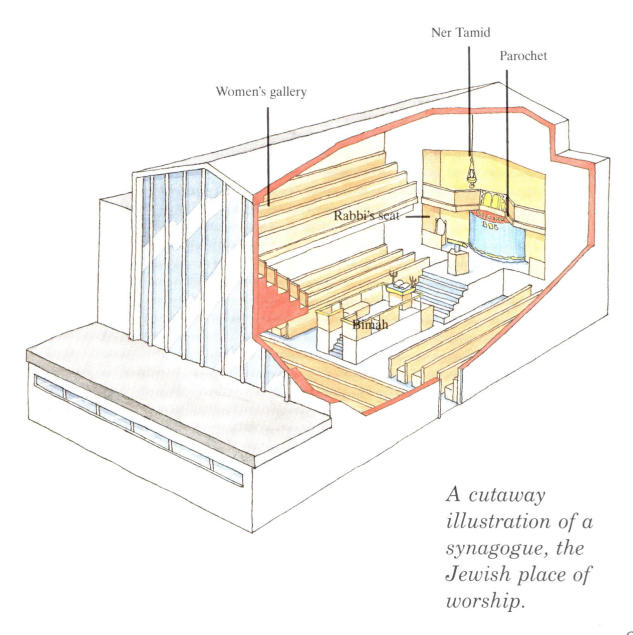

Ner Tamid

Parochet

Women's gallery

Rabbi's seat

Bimah

A cutaway illustration of a synagogue, the Jewish place of worship.

23

embroidered with religious symbols. They are mounted with a silver crown and bells and over the cover is a breastplate. This represents the High Priest's breastplate from the Temple in Jerusalem. The doors of the Ark are covered with a curtain called a *parochet*. Over this are two tablets which contain the

Inside a Jewish synagogue. The six-pointed Star of David, the Jewish symbol, is visible.

first two words of each of the Ten Command-
ments in Hebrew. Below it is written, 'Know
before whom you stand'.

To one side of the Ark stands a seven-
branched candlestick called a *menorah* and
nearby hangs a lamp, the *ner tamid*, which
burns constantly.

To one side of the Ark is a pulpit which is
used by the *rabbi* when speaking to the congregation. In the centre of the synagogue
stands the *bimah* from where the scrolls are
read during worship. In Orthodox (strict)
synagogues the elders of the congregation sit
around the *bimah* and the rest of the men
also sit downstairs. Upstairs is a gallery
reserved for women and children. In Reformed
synagogues men and women sit together.

The synagogue may be richly decorated and
have stained-glass windows. As Judaism does
not allow religious statues or pictures the
walls may be inscribed with texts from the
Tenakh in Hebrew.

*A stained-glass
window showing a*
menorah – *a seven
branched
candelabrum which
is used in Jewish
ceremonies.*

Sikhism

Sikh temples are called *gurdwaras* which means 'the Guru's door' or 'the house of the Guru'. Originally a *gurdwara* was a building which housed a copy of the Sikh Holy Book, the *Guru Granth Sahib*.

Sikh temples are often plain buildings on the outside only distinguished by the Sikh flag, the *Nishan Sahib*. This is yellow with a design of a double-edged sword, *khanda*, surrounded on each side by two, curved swords, *kirpans*. These are all enclosed in a circle, the *chakra*.

The *gurdwara* has three important rooms. The main room is the hall where people worship. In a central position towards the end wall of the room is the throne or *takht* where the copy of the *Guru Granth Sahib* is placed on a stool, the *Manjib Sahib*, which is covered with a silk cloth. Above it is a silk canopy

A reading of the Guru Granth Sahib *in the Golden Temple at Amritsar.*

26

called the *palki*. This all shows the importance which their Holy Book has in the religious life of Sikhs.

There is sufficient space around the *takht* for people to walk. In front of it there is a cloth on which the worshippers can place the gifts which they bring to the service and to the side is a place for the musicians to sit. They provide music for the hymns which are sung during the service. The floor of the hall

The Nishan Sahib, *the Sikh flag, is hoisted outside a* gurdwara *in London.*

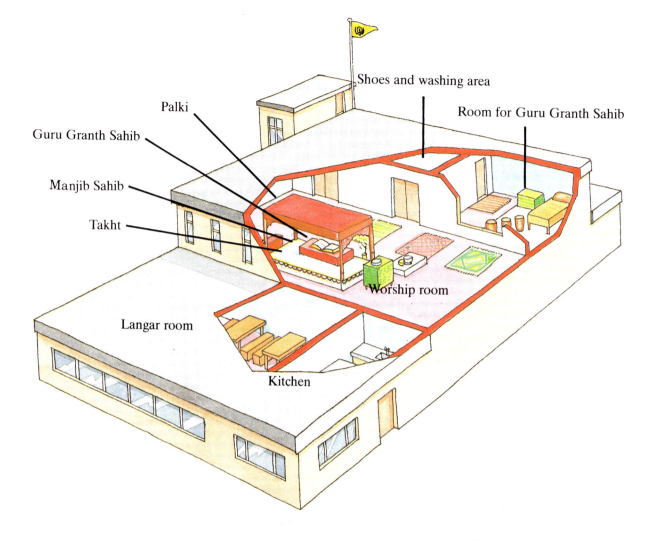

Palki

Shoes and washing area

Room for Guru Granth Sahib

Guru Granth Sahib

Manjib Sahib

Takht

Langar room

Worship room

Kitchen

is carpeted as people do not wear shoes there. Traditionally the women sit on the left and the men on the right. In a *gurdwara* everyone wears a headcovering and when seated they

A cutaway illustration of a Sikh gurdwara.

make sure that their feet are not pointing in the direction of the *Guru Granth Sahib*. The walls are decorated with pictures of the Sikh Gurus.

Somewhere usually higher than the main hall, is a smaller room in which the *Guru Granth Sahib* is kept during the night. The third room is the *langar* or Guru's kitchen where the free meal is prepared which is served to all worshippers after the service.

The most famous *gurdwara* is the Golden Temple at Amritsar which is in the Punjab state of India.

The most famous gurdwara *is the Golden Temple at Amritsar in the Punjab State of India.*

29

Glossary

Altar The table on which the Christian Holy Communion is celebrated.

Ardhamandapa The porch of a Hindu temple.

Baptism A Christian religious ceremony where a person is immersed or sprinkled with water as a sign that they are cleansed of sin and are now a member of the Church.

Bimah A raised platform in the centre of a synagogue from where services are conducted.

Imam A leader of a Muslim community.

Menorah A seven-branched candlestick.

Mihrab A recess in a mosque wall which tells the direction of prayer.

Muezzin The person who calls Muslims to prayer.

Nave The part of a church where people sit.

OM A Hindu religious symbol. It means eternal.

Pradakshina The passage around a Hindu shrine.

Qibla The wall of a mosque which faces Mecca and is the direction of prayer.

Swastika A Hindu symbol of good luck.

Tenakh Jewish Holy Scriptures.

Torah The first five books of the Jewish Bible.

Wudu The ritual washing before prayer in the Islamic religion.

Further Reading

If you would like to find out more about religious buildings, you may like to read the following books:

Beliefs and Believers series – published by Wayland
Exploring Religion series – published by Bell and Hyman
Religions of the World series – published by Wayland

Worship series – published by Holt Saunders.

Islam – produced by ILEA Learning Resources.
The Jesus Project – produced by CEM Video, 2 Chester House, Pages Lane, London N10.
Through the Eyes series – produced by CEM Video.

Acknowledgements

The Publisher would like to thank the following for providing the pictures for the book: Bruce Coleman Ltd 6, 10, 15, 18, 29; Sonia Halliday 11 (above) 17 (right), 19; Anne and Bury Peerless 14, 17 (left), 22, 26; David Richardson 27; Malcolm S. Walker 9, 12, 16, 21, 23, 28; Wayland Picture Library 4, 11 (left); Zefa 5, 7, 8, 13, 25.

Index